M1 IPAD PRO USER GUIDE

A Complete Step By Step Instruction
Manual For Beginners And Seniors To
Learn How To Use The New 11" & 12.9"
M1 Chip iPad Pro 2021 Model With
iPados 14.5 Tips And Tricks

BY

HERBERT A. CLARK

Table of Contents

INTRODUCTION

The iPad Pro is Apple's top-notch tablet. The latest iPad Pro model released in April 2021 features the M1 chip, a better front camera, Thunderbolt port, a Liquid Retina XDR mini-LED screen for the larger version, and about 16 GB RAM and 2 TB of storage space. In terms of design, the iPad Pro is unchanged and it is available in two sizes; 11 inches and 12.9 inches, and doesn't have a Home button.

Everything you need to know about making the most out of the 11-inch and 12.9-inch iPad Pro is covered in this guide

FEATURES OF THE M1 IPAD PRO

Design

The iPad Pro 2021 model did not have major design updates and is similar to the previous models. The 11-inch iPad Pro is 7.02 inches wide and 9.74 inches long, while the 12.9-inch version is 8.46 inches wide and 11.04 inches long.

The 11-inch iPad Pro is 5.9mm thick, while the 12.9-inch iPad Pro is about 6.4mm thick. The 11-inch iPad Pro weighs approximately 1.03 pounds, while the 12.9-inch iPad Pro weighs approximately 1.5 pounds.

The iPad 2020 continues to feature a 6mm bezel display on the top, bottom, and sides. The iPad Pro model shares the iPhone 12's industrial smooth ends.

The sleep/wake button, as well as two microphones, are situated on the top of the iPad Pro. On the right are the volume down and up buttons, the magnetic connector, and a nano-SIM tray. As with the foregoing models, the iPad Pro does not carry a headphone jack and requires a Bluetooth headset or USB-C-compatible headset.

A camera has, a wide-angle camera, full-angle camera, LiDAR scanner, and True Tone flash remain unchanged on the 2021 model.

The iPad Pro has a Thunderbolt / USB 4 port to charge the device and to connect with accessories.

Screen

Mini-LED Liquid Retina XDR screen

The Liquid Retina XDR screen on the 12.9-inch iPad Pro has a resolution of 2732 by 2048 and 264 pixels per inch. The iPad Pro's Liquid Retina XDR screen adds dynamic range to the device, resulting in a breathtaking visual experience

On the Apple iPad Pro, Apple's small LED display uses more than 10,000 LEDs behind the entire

display, creating a full brightness of up to 1000 nits, a large brightness of 1,600 nits, and a contrast ratio of 1 million-to-1. It captures the brightest details and subtle detail of the darkest images, allowing creators to see and edit HDR content in real-time on a large portable screen.

The Liquid Retina XDR screen features 120Hz ProMotion, True Tone, and free P3 color support.

LED liquid retina screen

The 11 -inch iPad Pro still features the liquid retina screen similar to the 2020 version.

The screen can provide a brightness of about 600 nits with only 1.8% reflectivity. It still has fingerprint-resistant and an antireflective coating

Compatibility with wide color provides clear colours that are accurate and true to life.

There's also ProMotion display technology, which has a 120Hz refresh rate, which makes the screen contents smoother, sharper, etc. making it more efficient for scrolling, playing games, watching movies, and more.

The update rate of the iPad Pro's display may vary depending on what's seen on the screen as an active and battery-saving device. The refresh rate is 120Hz when you watch movies or play games, but the 120Hz refresh rate is not required when you are reading a webpage or viewing pictures, it adjusts when needed.

TrueDepth camera system and Face ID

The iPad Pro utilizes the Face ID feature for unlocking and authenticating. Face ID does everything Touch ID does, like unlocking the iPad, giving access to a third-party password-protected application, confirming purchases, and confirm Apple Pay payments.

Face ID uses a sensor and camera built in the iPad Pro. To scan your face for authentication purposes, a dot projector would project more than 30,000 invisible infrared dots on your face.

An infrared camera reads the dot map and sends your face structure to the m1 chip on your device, where it gets transformed into a mathematical model.

The iPad Pro only takes a fraction of a second to scan through your face, get to know you, and unlock your device. A security feature known as **Attention Aware** ensures that your iPad Pro will open when you stare at it with your eyes open, so it won't work when there's no live person in its front.

Face ID info is encrypted and saved on the M1 chip Secure Encryption. The authentication takes place on your device with no data saved on the cloud, sent to Apple, or accessed by any application.

Apple has programed Face ID to function in the dark, when you put on sunglasses and cover the face with a beard, glasses, makeup, headbands, and other accessories. Face ID can also change with facial changes, so if you grow your beard or hair it will continue to know you.

On the iPad Pro, Face ID works in portrait or landscape orientation.

Selfie camera

The front TrueDepth camera system features a new 12-megapixel camera for FaceTime video, and selfies, it still compatible with Portrait lightning, Portrait mode, and Animoji & Memoji.

The new Ultra-Wide camera allows the Center Stage to keep users framed perfectly in video calls. The Center Stage utilizes the M1's machine learning capabilities to recognize and keep users in the middle of the frame

When the user moves around, the Center Stage moves automatically to keep them in the frame. When other individuals join the call, the camera also detects them and easily adjusts to fit everyone's appearance, and makes sure they're in conversation.

M1 Chip

The latest iPad Pro is the first iPadOS device to feature the M1 chip.

The M1 chip in the iPad Pro offers a number of specialized technologies, including Apple's next 16-core Neural engine and a more advanced ISP.

The M1 chip also lets your device support 2-times faster storage and store about 2TB of storage, and will also support a compact and high-end storage architecture with memory up to 16 GB. The previous model was only compatible with 1TB storage and 6 GB RAM.

LiDAR scanner and Rear camera

The iPad Pro features a 12-megapixel camera with an f / 1.8 driver, and an ultra-wide 10-megapixel camera that has a f / 2.4 driver s well as a 125-degree view field.

True Tone Flash, automatic image enhancement, intelligent HDR, 63-megapixel panoramas, burst mode, noise reduction, wide color capture, Live Photos support, and 5x digital zoom are all there. Like the 2018 and 2020 models, the 2021 iPad model does not have optical image enhancement.

Next to the two large cameras is the LIDAR Scanner (Light Detection and Change) that makes use of light reflected to measure distances up to five meters (16.4 feet) away from the iPad Pro.

The M1 ISP and the M1's Neural Engine make the camera system of the iPad pro more capable, bringing support for Smart HDR 3. The ISP and LiDAR Scanners can focus images and videos quickly and accurately in low-light conditions, capturing details with almost no light.

Battery life

The latest iPad Pro features an **all-day battery life** with a lifespan of about ten hours when you're navigating through the Internet or when you watch videos thanks to the M1 chip's performance.

The WiFi + Cellular version features a lifespan of nine hours when browsing the Internet using 5G.

Microphone and speakers

The iPad Pro has five studio -quality microphones to get the cleanest sound and the quietest detail.

Apple has designed the iPad Pro with four voice speakers that adjust the sound in all orientations. The iPad has two speakers on the top and two speakers on the bottom, which provide stereo sound.

5G connection

The iPad Pro Cellular model offers 5G connectivity to provide quicker data speeds while browsing.

The iPad Pro model in the US is compatible with millimeter wave, high frequency 5G version, which allows the device to reach wireless speeds of about 4Gbps. Other countries have slower sub 6GHz 5G connections.

The iPad Pro is also compatible with eSIM, which simplifies network access.

WiFi and Bluetooth compatibility

As with the foregoing models, the 2021 iPad Pro model is compatible with Bluetooth 5.0 and WiFi 6, also known as 802.11ax.

WiFi 6 devices are also compatible with WPA3, a security protocol that provides enhanced cryptographic power.

Storage and RAM

The iPad Pro storage space begins with 128 GB and can be upgraded to about 2TB of storage space.

The iPad Pro model with 128 GB, 256 GB, or 512 GB storage has 8 GB RAM, and the iPad Pro model with 1TB or 2TB storage has 16 GB RAM.

Thunderbolt

For the first time, the iPad Pro model will have Thunderbolt and USB 4 ports, which support 4x more bandwidth and 40 Gbps than the previous iPad Pro for wired connectivity.

Thunderbolt is compatible with 10Gbps Ethernet. The iPad Pro can support more peripherals and accessories and speeds faster than ever before.

The Smart connector

The smart connector allows your device to connect to power devices like the Smart Keyboard on the iPad Pro's back. The Smart Connector interface can transfer power and data, so the devices that connect to the iPad Pro don't need batteries.

SETUP YOU DEVICE

Getting ready to setup

To make setting up your device as easy as possible, ensure the following items are accessible:

- ❖ Internet connection via Wi-Fi or mobile data service via carrier (Wi-Fi + Cellular model)
- ❖ An Apple ID that belongs to you as well as the password; If you do not own an Apple ID, you can create one while setting up your device
- ❖ If you want to add a card to Apple Pay while setting up your device, you would need your credit or debit card account info
- ❖ If you transfer your data to a new device, you may need your old device or a backup of your iPad.
- ❖ If you want to transfer your Android content, you would need your Android device

Setting up your device

❖ Long press your iPad top button until the Apple icon shows.

Top button

When you switch on your first iPad Pro, you'll be greeted with "Hello" in different languages.

❖ To start, tap on the slide then slide your finger across the screen.
❖ Choose your language.
❖ Select your region or country.
❖ Select a Wi-Fi network. If you are not on Wi-Fi, you can configure it later. Select cellular rather.

❖ At this junction, you can decide to make use of **automatic set up** to configure your new device with the password and setting of your old iPad. If you decide to configure your device manually follow the steps below.

❖ After reading about Apple data and privacy info, click on the Continue button.

❖ Click the **Enable Location Services** button. If you do not want to activate location services while setting up your device, you can do it later, simply click on **Skip Location Services.**

❖ Adhere to the directives on your display to Set up Face ID.

❖ Then Create a password on your device. You can create a custom six-digit password, or you can create a four-digit passcode by clicking on the **password option**.

You would then be asked if you want to setup your device as new, restore from backup, or transfer info from android. If you want to setup as new, follow the guidelines below.

* Tap on the **setup as new iPad** button.
* Enter your Apple ID and login code. If you don't own an Apple ID, you can setup one for yourself while setting up your device. Simply click on Don't have an Apple ID? And adhere to the guidelines below.
* Read Apple's terms and conditions and agree to them.
* Click on Agree again to affirm.
* Configure Apple Pay.
* Configure iCloud Keychain.
* Configure Siri and Hey Siri.
* Click on **send diagnostics information to Apple** when there is a crash in an application or other problem, or click on **do not send** if you do not want to send.
* Enable **Display Zoom** to get more visual accessibility.
* Click on the Get Started button.

MOVE FILES FROM ANDROID DEVICE TO YOUR IPAD

Transferring your pictures, calendar, contacts, and accounts from your Android phone or tablet to your new iPad is easier with the Move to iOS application. Apple's first Android application connects old and new Apple devices with a direct Wi-Fi connection and transfers all your data. If the iOS app transfers most of your data, it does not transfer your application (due to incompatibility), music, or your passwords.

How to transfer your data from Android to iPad

❖ Setup your iPad pro till you get to the screen known as **Apps and Data**.

❖ Click on **Transfer data from Android**.

❖ Open the Google Play Store on your Android device and look for **Move to iOS**, then install the application.

❖ When you are done installing, select Open.
❖ On both devices, press the Continue key.
❖ Click on Accept and Next on your Android device.

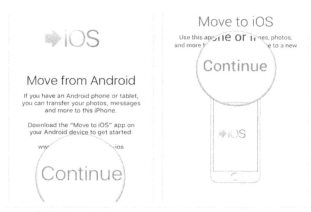

❖ Type the code shown on your iPad on your Android phone.

Once the code is entered, the Android device will be connected to your iPad via your p2p Wi-Fi connection and determine what information to transfer.

It would ask if you want to transfer your Google account information, Chrome notes, text messages, contacts and videos, and photos. Select what you want to copy.

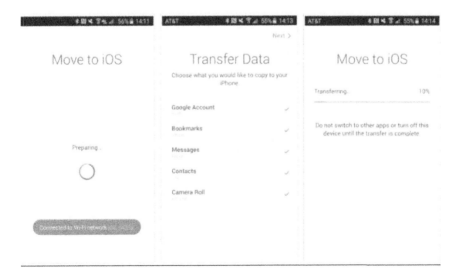

Your Android device would transfer the data you selected to your iPad. Both devices will be disconnected.

When the transfer is complete, click the **Continue setup on iPad** button on your iPad.

MOVE DATA FROM YOUR OLD IPAD TO YOUR NEW ONE

Apple has made it easy to move your info from your old device to a new one. Below is what you need to know about moving your info.

Using Automatic Setup

In iOS 11 and after, you can move your old device settings to your new one when you are physically close, and utilize it to setup the new iPad.

❖ On your new iPad, choose your language with your new and old devices close to each other.

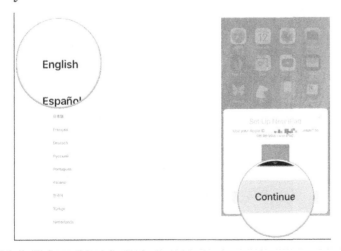

- ❖ Click the Continue button on your iPad with a pop-up menu show up, asking you setup your new iPad using your Apple ID.
- ❖ Use your old iPad to scan the picture that shows up on the new iPad.
- ❖ Enter the passcode of your old iPad into your new iPad.
- ❖ Setup Face ID on the new iPad.
- ❖ If this option appears, select restore your new iPad from your last backup.

- Pick whether to setup as a new iPad, restore your new iPad from an iTunes back up or iCloud back up, or move data from your Android gadget.
- Accept terms & condition.
- Click on the Continue button under the Express settings to utilize Siri settings, Find My device, Location, and analytics of usage now transferred from the old iPad.
- Finish the setup

Use iCloud

If you utilize iCloud to backup your device, you can transfer everything wirelessly to the new iPad. However, before doing so, you will want to backup your old iPad one last time to make sure you get everything on your new device as quickly as possible.

- Open the setting application on your old iPad
- Click on the Apple ID icon.
- Click on iCloud.

* ❖ Click on the iCloud backup.
* ❖ Now back up your device.

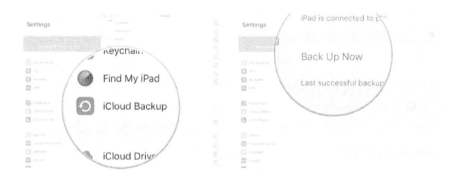

Once you have backed up your iPad, you will want to restore it to your new device.

* ❖ Start the setup process on your new device.

❖ Follow the initial setup guidelines. If you want to transfer everything from the old iPad to the new iPad, make use of automatic set up.

❖ Click on the **Restore from [latest iCloud back up date] backup** button to restore from your latest iCloud backup.

❖ Click on agree.

❖ Complete your new iPad setup.

BASIC SETTINGS

Basic Gestures

Tap: To touch your screen lightly with a finger

Press and hold: Tap and hold the item in an application to preview the content and take quick action. On the home screen, Press and hold the icon of an application to open the quick action menu.

Swipe: Quickly move a finger across your screen.

Zoom: put two of your fingers on your screen close to each other, without lifting them spread your fingers apart to zoom in, and move them close to each other to zoom out.

You can also double-click on a picture or web page to zoom in, and double-click once more to zoom out.

Go home: Swipe from the bottom part of your display to return to the home screen whenever you want.

Quick access to controls: Swipe down from the upper right part of the screen to launch the control centre; press and hold controls to display other options. Open the Setting application then click on control Centre to add controls or remove controls.

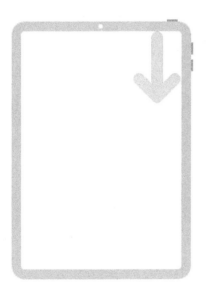

Launch the application switcher: simply swipe up from the bottom of your display and stop at the centre of your display, and then lift your finger.

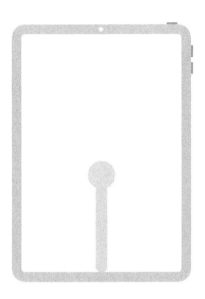

Switch between open applications: To move between open applications, swipe left or right at the bottom of your screen.

Ask Siri: simply Say, **Hey Siri**. Alternatively, hold down the top button and state your request. Siri listens till you release the button.

Use Accessibility shortcuts: Press the top button three times.

Capture a screenshot: Hold down the volume up key and the top button together and release them quickly.

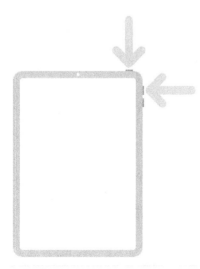

Shut down. Long Press the iPad's top button and the volume up button till the slide appears, then pull the slider to shut down your iPad. Or go to Settings click on General and tap on shut down.

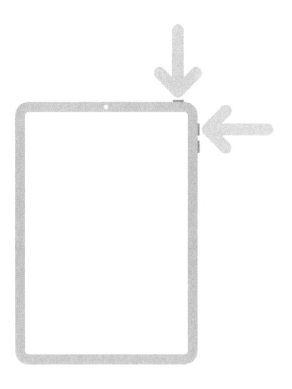

Utilize and personalize the Control Center on your iPad

The iPad's control center allows you to instantly access necessary controls such as flight mode, DND, flash lights, screen brightness, volume, and applications.

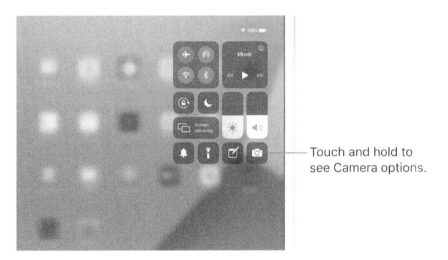

Touch and hold to see Camera options.

Launch the Control Centre

Simply Swipe down from the upper-right edge of the display. Swipe up back to close the control centre

Get access to more control in the control centre

Most controls offer extra options. To see options that are available, hold down a control. For instance, in the Control Center adhere to the directives below:

❖ Long press the upper left control groups, and then press the AirDrop button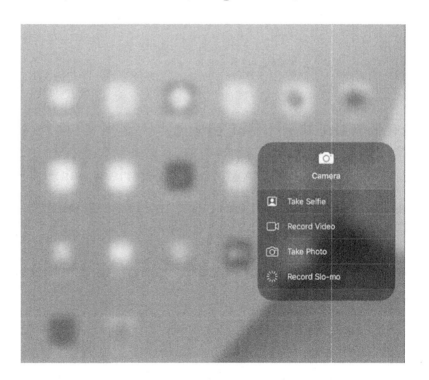 to open the AirDrop options.

❖ Long press the Camera button to scan a QR code, record a video, snap a selfie, etc.

Add and personalize controls

- ❖ Head over to the Settings application then tap on Control Center.
- ❖ To remove or add a control, click the add button ⊕ or the remove button ⊖ to a control.
- ❖ If you want to rearrange the control, click the Edit button ≡ beside a control and drag it to a new location.

Use search on iPad

On your iPad, Search is the best place to search for things. It can help you look for applications and contacts, search in applications such as Mail and Messages, look for and open web pages and start searching the Internet quickly.

You can choose the apps you plan on adding to search results. Research provides suggestions and results as you write.

Pick the applications to add to the search

❖ Run the Setting application after that tap on Siri and Search.

❖ Scroll down, click on an Application, then activate Show in Search.

Search on iPad

❖ Swipe down from the center of your home screen.

❖ Click the search box and type what you want.

❖ Do any of the below:

- Conceal the keyboard & display more results: press the Go button.

- launch an app that was suggested: click on the app.

- Find out more about search results: Search, then click one of the results to open it.

- Begin a new search: click the Delete button ⊗ in the search box.

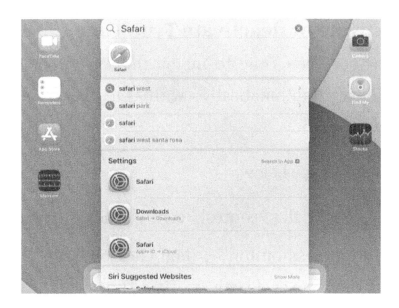

Disable search suggestions

❖ Launch the Settings application then click on Siri
and Search, after that disable search suggestions.

Disable location services for suggestions

Head over to the Settings application then click on
Privacy after that tap on Location Services.

Click System services, then disable Location-based
suggestions.

Activate or deactivate True Tone

Activate True Tone to match the screen color and intensity automatically with the light in the environment.

Do any of the below:

❖ Launch the control centre, hold down the Brightness button ☼, then click on True Tone ☀ to activate or deactivate True Tone.

❖ Head over to Settings then tap on Display and Brightness, then activate or deactivate true tone.

Activate or deactivate Night Shift

You can manually enable the Night Shift feature, which helps when you are in a dark room during the day.

Launch the control centre, hold down the Light button ☼, and then press the Night Shift button ☾

Setup Night Shift to automatically activate or deactivate

Use Night Shift to rotate the colors on the screen to the spectrum warmer end at night and it will be easier for your eyes to view the screen.

❖ Head over to the Settings application then tap on Display and Brightness after that click on Night shift.

❖ Activate scheduled

❖ To adjust the color balance in Night Shift, slide the slider to the warm or cold end below the color temperature.

❖ Click on From, and then choose from sunset to sunrise or click on Custom Schedule then follow the guidelines on your screen to complete the setup

Set time and date on your device

As a rule, the date and time displayed on the Lock screen are immediately determined depending on your location. If it doesn't go wrong, you can fix it.

❖ Head over to Settings then click on General after that tap on Date and Time.

❖ Activate any of the below:

- Automatically set: The iPad takes the exact time of your network and updates it for your region. Some networks do not support network time, so in some countries or regions, local time may not be set by the iPad.

- 24-hour time: The iPad displays 0 to 23 hours.

Activate or deactivate dark mode

The dark mode gives the iPad a dark color scheme that meets the lighting conditions for low-light environments. You can activate the dark mode from the control centre or schedule it to automatically activate at night. As long as the dark mode is enabled, you can utilize your device, for example, to read in bed without worrying about disturbing the people around you.

Do one of the below:

❖ Launch the control center, press and hold the Light button ☼, and then press the Screen button ◐ to activate or deactivate Dark Mode.

❖ Head over to the Settings application then click on Display and Brightness and then choose Dark to turn on the dark mode or light to activate light and turn the dark mode off.

Take a screenshot on your iPad

You can take a screenshot to share with others or use it in a document.

- ❖ Simultaneously Press then release the top key of your device and the volume up key.
- ❖ Tap on the screen shot on the lower-left part, and then click on done.
- ❖ Click on store the image, store it to Files, or delete this Screen shot.

If you choose to store to photos, you would see it in the Screen shot album in the photo application.

Capture a full-page screenshot

You can capture a full-page, scrolling screen shot of a web page, documents, or emails that are longer than the length of the iPad screen. Screenshots are stored in PDF format.

- ❖ Simultaneously Press then release the top key on your device and the volume up key.

- ❖ Click on the screenshot in the bottom left part of your screen, then click on full page.
- ❖ Do one of the following:
  - Store the screenshot: click on done, select save the PDF to Files, select a location, and then click on Save.
  - Share a screenshot: click on the Share button ⬆️, select a sharing option, enter any other required information, and send it.

Change the screen orientation on your iPad

You can lock the orientation of your screen so that it does not change when your iPad is rotated.

- ❖ Simply Launch the Control Center, then touch the Lock orientation buttons 🔄.
- ❖ When the display orientation is locked, the Orientation Lock icon would show up on the status bar.

Create a screen record

You can create a screen record and record audio on the iPad.

❖ Head over to the Settings application then click on Control Center, then click on beside to screen recording.

❖ Launch the control centre, then tap on the record button , and then wait for a three-second count down.

❖ To end the recording, launch the Control Center, click on , or the red line at the top of the screen, and click on the Stop button.

❖ Head over to the photos application, then choose the screen recording.

Remove or add a keyboard on iPad

You can enable or disable typing features like spellings checking on your iPad, modify your onscreen or wireless keyboard layout, and more.

If you add a keyboard for another language, you can type on both languages without switching between keyboards

To remove or add a keyboard, simply adhere to the guidelines below:

❖ Run the Setting app, then tap on the General button after that tap on Keyboard.

❖ Click on keyboards, and do any of the below:

- Add keyboard: simply click on the **Add New Keyboard** option. Repeat this step to add more keyboard

- Remove a keyboard: Click on edit then tap on the minus button⬤ beside the keyboard you plan to remove, then click on delete and tap on done.

- Rearrange keyboard list: click on the edit option, then drag≡ beside a keyboard to another place in the catalogue, after that click on done.

If you add a keyboard for different languages, it is automatically added to the preferred language list. You can see this list as well as add languages directly to it by opening the settings application, then click on General after that tap on Language and Region.

Move to another keyboard

❖ On the keyboard in your screen: long press ⊕ or
   ☺, then click on the keyboard name you want to switch to

   You can still click on ☺ or ⊕ to move from one keyboard to a different keyboard. Keep clicking to access other activated keyboards

Schedule Dark mode to automatically activate and deactivate

❖ Head over to the Setting application, then tap on Display and Brightness.
❖ Enable Automatic, then click on Options.
❖ Choose Sunset to Sunrise or Custom Schedule.

If you select a custom schedule, click on the option to set the time you want for the dark mode to activate or deactivate.

If you choose Sunset to sunrise, the iPad utilizes your clock and geolocation data to determine when the night will be for you.

Display the remaining battery percentage on the status bar

Launch the Settings application then click on Battery, after that activate battery percentage.

Open an application on Slide Over on your iPad

You can utilize an application that slides in another application's front. For example, when making use of Maps, launch the messages application in Slide over to continue the conversation.

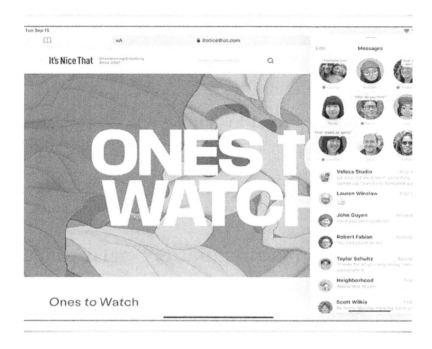

Ones to Watch

The iPad tracks the apps you open with Slide Over, so you can easily switch between them.

To do this:

❖ First, ensure you have at least tone application open.

❖ Open the dock on your iPad by swiping slowly up from the end of the screen. Don't do it quickly, or you may enter the Home Screen accidentally.

❖ Look for the Application You Want to utilize with slide over from the dock. Long press the icon of the application for a second, then slowly drag it to the left or the right part of your iPad's screen. Do not go to the right edge or the left edge, or you would open split view.

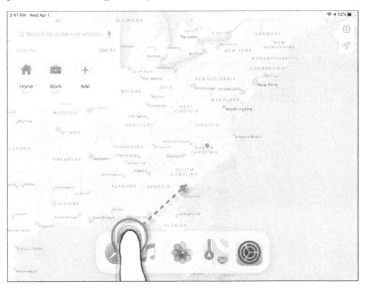

The application would show in the slide-over window on the right or the left of your display.

To change the location of the window, Put your finger on the window for a second and drag it to the part of the screen you want.

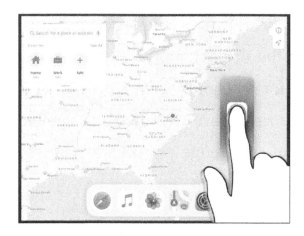

To close the slide-over window put your finger on the gray line and swipe it to the closest screen edge.

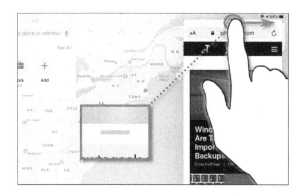

How to use slide over with two applications open

You can utilize Slide over for multitasking with two applications open in slide view.

Open two applications in split view to begin. Then pull the new application to the middle of the application divider. Raise your finger and the third application will show in the middle.

Delete applications from iPad

❖ Tap and hold the application you want to delete to open the quick action menu, then click on Delete application.

If the apps start jiggling, click the delete button
× on the app you plan on deleting.

Multitask using picture in picture

You can utilize Facetime or watch a movie while utilizing other applications

Click the restore down button⌐⊻⌐ when making use of facetime or watching a video.

The video window will restore down to one corner of the screen. You can see other open apps and find other programs. With the video playing in the window you can do any of the below:

❖ Change the size of the video window: pinch open and pinch close to change the size.
❖ Display and hide control: touch the window of the video.
❖ Move video window: pull or drag it to another location on your screen.
❖ Close your video window: Press the Cancel button ⊗ .
❖ Go back to a full video screen or FaceTime screen: Tap the maximize button ⬚ in a small window.

How to make use of drag-and-drop on your device

Slide over and split view are not only useful for comparing notes but They can also be used to share info between two applications. To do this:

- ❖ Launch two applications in split view or slide view.
- ❖ Highlight a segment of the text from an application.
- ❖ Place a finger on the highlighted text and drag it to the application open on the other part of the split view.
- ❖ Raise your finger. The text you dragged would show up in the other application.

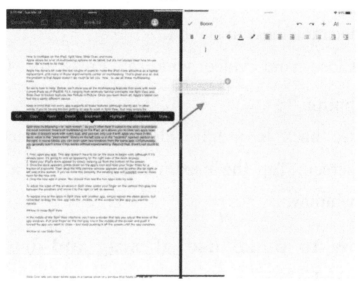

Open two applications in Split View on your iPad

Launch two applications or two windows from one application by dividing the screen into resizable views. For instance, open the messages application and the maps app in Split View at the same time. Alternatively, open two message windows in Split View and manage two conversations at once.

To do this:

❖ First of all, you need to ensure that one of the applications you want to open is in your Dock already. To do this, open the application you want and close it so that it appears in one of the **newly used application** areas of the Dock.

❖ Once you make sure that the application is in the Dock, open the other application you want to utilize and keep the application open.

❖ Swipe up gently from the bottom of your screen and stop at the middle, to open the dock.

Drag to resize the split.

❖ Hold down the application on the dock, then pull the application to the left or right edge of your display, then release.

If two things are already open in Split View, drag one over the other to replace it.

Drag the application divider to the middle of your display to give the two views the same space.

Close the split view

Drag the application divider to the right or left side of your screen, depending on the application you are closing.

Using text replacement

Setup text replacement you can utilize to enter a phrase or a word by simply typing few characters. For instance, type the word **omw** to enter **on my way.**

Create your text replacement

❖ Do any of the below:

- On an on-screen keyword: long press on 😊 or 🌐 button, then click on keyboard setting, after that click on Text Replacement.

- Using an external keyboard: head over to Settings, then click on General after that tap on Keyboard, then click on Text Replacement.

❖ Tap on the add key╋ at the upper right part of your display

❖ Write the sentence on the sentence field and the shortcut text you want to utilize for it In the Shortcut field.

Use AirDrop on your iPad to send stuff to nearby devices

With AirDrop, you can transfer images, videos, web pages, your location, and more to other closeby devices and Macs (iOS 7, iPadOS 13, OS X 10.10, or after). AirDrop transmits data via both Wi-Fi and Bluetooth, which you need to be activated. To utilize AirDrop, you need to sign in with an Apple ID. The transmission is encrypted for security purposes.

Send things via AirDrop

- Open item you are sending, then click on the share button⬆, share, AirDrop button, More options button•••, or another button that shows the app sharing options

- Click on the AirDrop icon ◉ in the share options row, then click on the AirDrop user profile picture close to you.

If the individual does not show up as an AirDrop user nearby, ask him or her to open the Control Center on an iPod touch, iPad, or iPhone and let Airdrop receive items. To send to people using Mac, tell them to let themselves be discovered in AirDrop in the Finder.

Let others send things to your iPad via AirDrop

❖ Launch the control center, long-press the upper-left control groups, and then click the AirDrop icon ◉.

❖ Just click on Everybody or Contacts to select the people you want to get items from.
You can accept or reject each request.

Set DND on your iPad

To silence your iPad fast, Whether you are having an evening or going to bed to keep your iPad quiet simply activate DND (Do Not Disturb). It mutes calls and notifications and stops them from flashing your screen.

Activate DND

Tell Siri. You could Say: **Turn on Do Not Disturb**

❖ Open the Control Centre and then click on the DND mode button 🌙 to activate it.

When DND is active, the DND button 🌙 appears on the status bar.

❖ To create a time to end the DND, long press the DND button 🌙 in the control center, and then select an option such as **1 hour** or **till this event end**. You can click on Schedule as well, activate Scheduled, and then set the time you want it to start and end.

Receive calls when DND is active

❖ Head over to the Settings application then click on Do Not Disturb.

❖ Do any of the below:

• Click on the **allow class from** button: to let Wi-Fi and Facetime call coming in from a selected group.

• Activate repeated calls: Allow the same caller to make an emergency call.

Permit emergency calls when DND is active

When DND is active you can allow call and message from emergency contact.

❖ Open the contacts application.

❖ Choose a contact, and then click on Edit.

❖ Tap Text Tone or Ring Tone, then enable the Emergency Bypass option.

Arrange silent hours

- ❖ Run the Setting application, then touch Do Not Disturb.
- ❖ Activate Schedule, then put the start time and time it would end.

Measure someone's height with your iPad

You can utilize the Measure application to measure someone's height from the top of the person's head to the floor. You can also measure the seated height of the person in the chair.

- ❖ Open the Measure application then arrange the iPad so that the individual you plan to measure shows in the iPad screen from head to toe.

A line would show up at the person's head, hair, or hat, and the measurement of the person's height would show under the line.

- ❖ Tap on the **Take Picture** key ◯ to take a photo.

❖ To save the image, click on the screenshot in the lower left part of your screen, then click on the Done button, and then select Save Images or Save to Files.

You can access and share the height measurement photos or files on your iPad at any time.

Pair the magic keyboard with your iPad

You can use the Magic Keyboard, the numeric keypad, and the Magic Keyboard to enter text on the iPad. The keyboard connects to the iPad pro with Bluetooth.

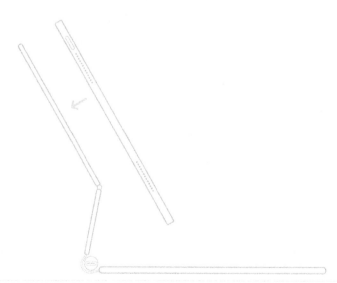

❖ Go to the Setting application and tap on Bluetooth and turn Bluetooth on.
❖ When the device shows up in the catalogue of Other Devices, choose the device.

Note: If the magic keyboard is already connected to other devices, you must disconnect the Magic Keyboard before connecting it to the iPad.

BACKUP IPAD

Backup your iPad via iCloud

❖ Head over to the Settings application then click on [your name]> iCloud then tap on iCloud backup.

❖ Activate iCloud backup. iCloud would back up your device automatically when it is connected to power, on WiFi, or locked

❖ Tap on the Back up Now option to manually back up your iPad.

To see your iCloud backups head over to the Settings application then click on [your name] after that tap on iCloud, click on Manage Storage, click on backup. To delete a backup, select the backup from the catalogue and click on Delete Backup.

Backup iPad via Mac

❖ Connect your iPad and computer via cable.

❖ Select iPad in the sidebar of the Finder on your Mac.

MacOS 10.15 or later is required to use Finder to get your iPad backed up. Use iTunes to backup your iPad with the previous macOS.

❖ Click on the **General** option at the Finder window top.

❖ Choose **Backup all the data in your iPad to this mac**.

❖ To encrypt the data you have backed up and store it using a passcode, choose **Encrypt Local Back up**.

❖ Tap on Backup Now.

Backup your iPad with a Windows computer

❖ Connect your device and computer via cable.

❖ In the iTunes application on your computer, click on the iPad button on the upper left side of the iTunes window.

❖ Tap on the Summary button.

- ❖ Tap on Backup Now (under back up)
- ❖ If you want to encrypt your back up, choose **Encrypt local backup**, enter your password, and tap on Set Passcode.

To view the back up that have been stored on your pc, tap on Edit then click on Preference and click Devices. The catalogue of Encrypted backups has a lock icon.

UPDATE IPAD

Your data and settings will not change when you upgrade to the latest version of the iPad.

Before you update it, setup your iPad to automatically backup, or manually backup your iPad

Automatically update your iPad

If you did not activate automatic updates when you setup your iPad for the first, adhere to the guidelines below:

❖ Run the Setting app and tap on General then touch Software Updates.
❖ Click on the personalize Automate Updates button (Automatic Update). You can download and install updates automatically.

When there is an update, the update is downloaded and installed on the iPad overnight when you are charging it and it needs to be connected to Wi-Fi.

You will be notified before an update will be installed.

Manually update your device

You can observe if there are any software updates and install available ones at any time.

❖ Run the Setting application and touch General then touch Software Update.

The display would show the recently installed version of the iPadOS and if there are any updates.

To deactivate automatic updates, launch the Settings application then click on General after that tap on Software updates then click on Automatic update (or customize automatic update).

CENTER STAGE

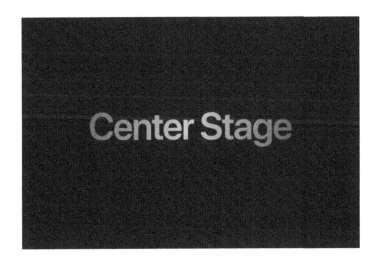

One of the things Apple announced during the Spring event in April 2021 was the latest new camera for the iPad Pro Called the Center Stage, it allows you to walk hand free and do other things while on a video call because it will always follow you to ensure you are in frame.

What is the center stage and how does center stage work?

According to Apple, the Center Stage makes use of the 12-megapixel TrueDepth camera of the iPad Pro, as well as the machine learning technology, to identify and keep the users in the middle. That way, the iPad Pro will pan the camera to automatically keep you in the frame even when you are moving around in a video call.

If others join the video call, the Center Stage will also accept them and zoom away to suit everyone.

Does Center Stage only work with FaceTime?

No. Apple stated it would work with third-party applications like Zoom and Webex, as well as FaceTime, and will soon have APIs for other applications.

Which Apple devices support the center stage?

The Center Stage only works for the 2021 iPad Pro.

FAMILY SHARING

Using family sharing, family members can share subscriptions, purchases, iCloud storage plans, etc. all without sharing an account.

To utilize family sharing, an adult family member (organizer) selects the features for the family group and would invite five other people to be part of the group. When members are added, Family Sharing is configured automatically on their devices.

Setup family sharing

Family Sharing demands that you (organizer) login with an Apple ID and verify the Apple ID you utilize for the Apple Books, iTunes Store, and Application Store.

❖ Head over to the Settings application then click on [your name] after that tap on Family sharing and adhere to the guidelines on the screen to create a family sharing group.

You can add members of your family or create a child account.

❖ Click on what you want to share, then adhere to the guidelines on your screen.

For more info on family sharing, adhere to the directives below:

- iCloud storage plan and subscriptions: You can share Application Store subscriptions, Apple subscriptions, and iCloud storage.

- Purchase: you can share your purchases on Apple TV, iTunes Store, Apple Books, and Application Store.

- Location: after sharing your location with members of the family, you can make use of the Find My application to find your location and help you find a lost device.

- Features for Kids: You can control your kid's spending and their use of Apple devices.

Add a family member

A family group organizer can add people to the family group.

❖ Head over to the Settings application then click on [your name], after that tap on Family Sharing, and then click on the Add Member button.

❖ Tap on Invite People, then adhere to the directives on your display.

You can send invitations via AirDrop, Messages, or Mail. If you are with a family member, you can click on **Invite in Person** and tell them to enter their Apple ID and passcode on the display known as **Family Members Apple ID**.

Create an Apple ID for a kid

Parents, guardians, or the family sharing organizer can generate an Apple ID for a kid in the Family Sharing group.

❖ Launch the Settings application then click on [your name] after that tap on Family sharing.

❖ Do any of the below:

- If you are the family group organizer: click the Add Member button, click Create Account for Child, and adhere to the guidelines on the screen.

- If you are a guardian or a parent: click on the Add Child button and adhere to the guidelines on the screen.

See what you share with your family

You can view what you share with your family and customize your sharing settings whenever you like. Things you share with your family group would be displayed above those you do not share.

❖ Run the Setting application, and tap on [your name] after that tap on Family sharing.

❖ Click on a feature, after that do one of the below:

- If you have not already setup the feature: adhere to the directives on your display.

- If you have setup the feature: Review and modify the feature if you want.

Activate the Ask To Buy feature for kids

When you create a family sharing group, the organizer of the group may decide to turn on the **Ask To Buy** feature so that the children in the family group would ask for permission to buy or downloads things. Purchases can be approved by the organizer, parent, or guardian of the group.

❖ Run the Setting application, and tap on [your name] after that click on Family sharing.

❖ Click on Ask To Buy, then do any of the below:

- If you do not have children in your family group: click on Add a child or Create A Child Account then adhere to the guidelines on your screen

- If you have a child in your family group: click on the name of the child and activate Ask To Buy.

Note: The age limit for Ask To Buy varies by region. In the United States, a family sharing group organizer can activate Ask To Buy for members of the family below the age of 18; For children under 13, it is activated by default.

Setup Screen Time with Family Sharing on your device

You can setup screen time for your children through family sharing. These include downtime, application use allowance, contacts your kids communicate with, ratings for contents, etc. The screen time allows you and your kid to see how they are making use of their devices and to use that information to plan for their use.

❖ Head over to the Settings application then click on [your name] after that click on Family section> Screen time.

❖ Click on the family member's name, then activate screen time, and then adhere to the guidelines on your screen.

Stop sharing purchases with your family members on your iPad

The organizer of a family sharing group can activate purchase sharing. Any purchases by the members of the family sharing group in the Apple TV, Apple Books, iTunes Store, and Application Store are paid for with the Apple ID account of the organizer.

If adults and teenagers in the family sharing group do not want to share purchase and payment info with other family members, they can deactivate this feature.

❖ Head over to the Settings application then tap on [your name] after that click on Family sharing.
❖ Click on the Purchase Sharing button, and disable the **Share purchase with your family** option.

If the organizer wants to deactivate the Purchase haring feature completely, he can click on Stop Purchasing Sharing.

Setup Apple Cash Family on iPad (US only)

Organizers of the family sharing group can setup an Apple Cash accounts for children in the family group and utilize the Wallet application on the iPhone to check card balances, monitor transactions, and limit to whom the child can send money.

- ❖ Run the Setting application> [your name] then click on Family sharing.
- ❖ Click on Apple Cash, then do any of the below:
  - If you do not have children in your family group: click on **Add a child** or create **Child account**, then adhere to the guidelines on your screen

- If you have a child in your family group: click on the name of the child, click on **Setup Apple Cash**, and adhere to the guidelines on your screen.

Disable or leave a Family Sharing group

❖ Head over to the Settings application, then click on [your name] after that tap on Family sharing, click on [your name].

❖ Do any of the below:

- Dissolve the family sharing groups: click on Stop using family. Only the group organizer has the power to dissolve the group.

- Leave the family sharing group: click on Stop using family sharing.

Little kids can't remove themselves from the group and must be transferred to another family before disbanding your own.

SIRI

Speaking to Siri is a fast means to get things done on the iPad. Ask Siri to translate sentences, set timers, look for a location, get weather reports, etc. The more you utilize Siri the better it knows your needs.

To utilize Siri, your iPad needs to be connected to the Internet.

Response from Siri

Tap to continue speaking to Siri.

Setup Siri

If you did not setup Siri when you set up your iPad, head over to the Settings application, click on Siri and Search, and do any of the below:

- ❖ If you want to call Siri using your voice: activate listen for **Hey Siri**.
- ❖ If you want to call Siri using the top button: activate press Top button for Siri.

Call Siri with your voice

When you call Siri with your voice, Siri replies loudly.

- ❖ Just say **Hey Siri** and state your request or tell Siri to perform a task.
  For instance, you can state something like Hey Siri, how is today's weather? or Hey Siri set an alarm for 12 pm.
- ❖ To ask another question or do something else, say **Hey Siri** once more or click on the Listen button.

Note: To stop the iPad from replying to **Hey Siri**, put the iPad face down or turn it off in settings.

Call Siri using a button

❖ Hold down the top button.

❖ When Siri shows up, state your request

Make adjustments if Siri doesn't get your request

Do any of the below

❖ Click the Listen button, then state your request in a different way.

❖ Click the Listen button, then repeat your request by spelling some of the words that Siri does not understand. For instance, say **Call** and spell the name of the person.

❖ Edit the message before it is sent: Say change it

Write rather than talking to Siri

❖ Head over to the Settings application> Accessibility> Siri, then activate Type to Siri.

❖ Call Siri to ask a question, then use the keyboard on your screen and text box to write your request.

Announce calls using Siri on your device

Siri detects incoming FaceTime calls with Announce calls, which you can accept or reject via your voice. It also works with compatible third-party applications.

- Head over to the Settings application, click on Siri and search then tap on Announce Call, and then select headset and car, Always or headset only.
- When the call arrives, Siri identifies the caller. State something like Hey Siri, answer that call or reject/decline the call.

  If your device is plugged into a compatible headset, Siri would ask if you would like to answer the call. Say yes or no.

APPLE PENCIL 2

Pairing the Apple Pencil 2

❖ Ensure your iPad on and open.

❖ Put the Apple pencil on the magnetic side of your iPad.

❖ When the Bluetooth pairing request shows up, click on the Pair button.

Charge the Apple Pencil

❖ Ensure Bluetooth is active on your device.

❖ Put the Apple Pencil in the magnetic connector on the right part of your device.

Utilize the Apple Pencil to insert text into any text field on your iPad

❖ Write using Apple Pencil in a text field and Scribble will help you to convert your handwriting into typed text automatically.

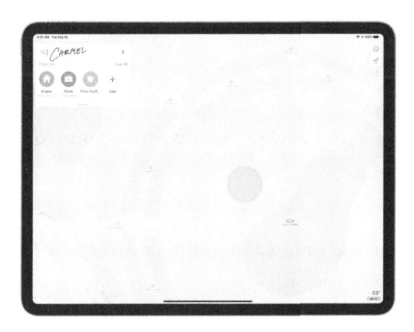

❖ Click on the Scribble bar to use the shortcut.

Utilize Apple Pencil to insert text into notes

❖ In the notes, click the Markup Switch button Ⓐ to display the markup tool bar.

- In the tool bar, click the Manuscript tool (left side of the pen).
- Use the Apple Pencil to write and Scribble would change what you have written with the pencil to text.

Select and review the text with your Apple Pencil

When you write a text with your Apple Pencil and Scribble, you can:

- Delete a word: scratch the word with your Apple Pencil.
- Enter text: long press a text field, then write on the text field that shows up.
- Select text: draw a circle around it, or you can underline the text to select and see options for editing.
- Select a word: double-click on it

❖ Select a paragraph: tap on a word in the paragraph three times, or drag Apple Pencil over the paragraph.

Stop changing your handwriting into text

Head over to the Settings application then click on Apple Pencil and deactivate Scribble.

Take a screenshot on your iPad and mark it up with Apple Pencil

You can utilize the Apple Pencil to quickly capture the iPad screen, then share it with others, or utilize it in a doc

❖ To take a picture of your screen, swipe up from any corner at the bottom of your iPad screen with your Apple Pencil.

❖ Draw with Apple Pencil to mark up your screenshots.

Use the Markup bar that is the lower part of your display to switch the drawing tools.

❖ To send the screenshot that you marked up to someone else (like in a message) or to save it in a file (like in a note), click the Share button⬆, then select an option.

❖ When you are done, press the done button, and then select an option.

CAMERA

Learn how to take nice pictures with the camera on your iPad. Select from camera modes like Square, Pano, and Photo, and utilize camera features like Live and Burst pictures.

Take a picture

Photo is the custom mode you see when you turn the camera on. Use Photo mode to take pictures. Select other modes, such as Video, Pan, Timelapse,

Slo-mo, and Portrait, by swiping the mode selector down or up.

- ❖ Click on the camera application on the Home screen, or swipe to the left on your iPad Lock screen to launch the Camera.
- ❖ Press the Shutter key or volume keys to snap the picture.

Press the Flash button⚡ to turn the light on or off, and then select Auto, On, or Off.

To adjust the timer, stabilize the iPad and arrange what you want to snap. Press the timer button⏱, then press 3s or 10s.

Note: When using the camera, a green dot shows up at the top of your display for your protection.

Take a Pano picture
- ❖ Select pano mode, then click on the Shutter button.

❖ Slowly move in the arrow direction, keeping it in the middle line.

❖ After panning, tap on the Shutter button once more to finish.

Tap the arrow to pan on the opposite side. To vertically pan, arrange your device orientation to landscape.

Take a selfie

❖ Navigate to the front camera by pressing the camera selector button⊙ or ▢ .

❖ Place the iPad in your front.

❖ Press the Shutter button or volume keys to snap the picture.

Take a selfie in portrait mode

This effect keeps the face sharp while you create a blurred beautiful background.

❖ Choose portrait mode.
  The front camera is on.
❖ Place yourself in the yellow box
❖ Tap on the Shutter key to take the photo.

Modify portrait lightning in portrait selfie

You can use studio lighting for Portrait Mode selfies.

❖ Choose Portrait mode.
❖ To select the lighting effect, drag the Portrait Lighting control button ⬡ :
  • Natural light: the face will be sharply focused against the blurred background.

- Studio Lighting: the face will be lit brightly, and the picture will have a clean look.
- Contour Lighting: the face will have a great shadow with lowlight and highlight.
- High-Key Light Mono: it creates a gray theme on a white background
- Stage lighting.
- Stage Light Mono: the result is the same as Stage Light, but the image is white and black.

❖ Tap on Shutter to snap a picture.

Adjust depth control in portrait mode selfie

Utilize the Depth Control slider to modify the level of blurriness in the background in your portrait selfies

❖ Select portrait mode, then arrange yourself for the selfie.

❖ Click the Adjust Depth button 🌀 on the right part of your display.

The depth control slide would appear on the right part of your screen.

❖ Move the slider down or up to adjust the effect.
❖ Tap on the Shutter key to take the photo.

Take burst photos

The burst mode captures multiple high-speed pictures so that you can choose from the different photos range. You can capture Burst pictures using the back and front cameras.

❖ Select square or photo mode.
❖ Press and hold the Shutter button to photos quickly.
The counter indicates the number of pictures you have taken.
❖ Raise your fingers to stop.
❖ Click the Burst thumbnail to select the pictures you want to store and then tap on the Select option.

The gray dots at the bottom of the thumbnails indicate the images submitted for storage.

❖ Touch the circle in the lower-right part of the picture you plan on saving as a different picture, and then click on done.

Delete the whole segment of Burst images by clicking the thumbnail, and click on Delete.

Take live photos

Live Image captures what happens before and after your image, including sound.

❖ Select Photo mode.

❖ Click on the live image button ◎ to activate the mode or turn it off (yellow light is on).

❖ Tap on Shutter to snap a photo.

Record a video

❖ Select Video mode.

❖ Press record, or press any of the volume keys to begin to record.

Pinch out or in to zoom.

❖ Press the record key, or press the volume key to end the recording.

Record a slo-mo video

❖ Select Slo-mo mode.

❖ Press the record button or the volume up button to start to record and also to end it.

To play a part of the video in Slo-mo and play the rest at normal speed, click on the thumbnail and then click Edit. Move the vertical bar at the bottom of the frame viewer to determine the segment you plan on playing in slo-mo.

To edit the Slo-mo recording setting, select Settings then click on Camera, and then tap on Slo-mo.

Take a video of the past

❖ Select the time-lapse mode.

- Place your device where you want to record the time-lapse video, for example, traffic flowing, sunrise, etc.
- To record, press the Record key; tap on it once more to stop.

Adjust the Auto FPS setting

The iPad can automatically reduce the frame rate to 24 fps and improve video quality in low-light situations.

Head over to the Settings application, then click on Camera, after that tap on Record Video, activate Auto Low Light FPS

Straighten your shot with a grid

To show a grid on the camera screen that will enable you to compose and straighten the shot you are about to take, head over to the settings application then click on Camera, after that activate Grid

Adjust the volume of the shutter

Adjust the camera shutter volume by making use of the volume buttons. Or when the camera is open, swipe down from the upper-right part of your screen to launch the control centre, then dag the volume slider ◀)).

Capture an HDR picture

High Dynamic Range helps to take beautiful pictures in high-contrast conditions. The iPad camera captures three pictures at high-speed at different exposures and mixes them. The picture that comes out from it would have better detail in midtone and bright areas.

iPad makes use of HDR when it is most effective.

To control HDR manually, head over to the Setting application then tap on camera, after that disable Smart HDR. When you are on the camera screen, click on HDR to activate it or deactivate it

Share pictures

❖ Click the share button ⬆, when viewing a picture,

❖ To share your photos, select the option which includes Message, Mail, Airdrop.

Scan a QR code with iPad Camera

You can utilize your iPad camera to scan a QR code for link to coupon, application, website, ticket, etc. The camera detects and highlights the QR code automatically.

❖ Simply launch the camera, then arrange the iPad in a way that the code shows on the screen.

❖ Click on the information that shows on the screen to enter the application or site.

FACETIME

You make voice and video calls to family and friends in the facetime application, whether they are making use of an iPod touch, iPad, a mac, or an iPhone. You can talk face to face with them using the front camera and use the back camera to show what you see around you

* Enter the setting application touch facetime then activate FaceTime.
* If you want to be able to capture live photos while a facetime call is going on, simply activate FaceTime Live Photo.
* Enter your email address, Apple ID, or phone number to utilize FaceTime.

Make FaceTime calls on your iPad

With an Internet connection and an Apple ID, you can call and get calls on FaceTime (you can first

login using your Apple ID or generate an Apple ID if
you do not own one).

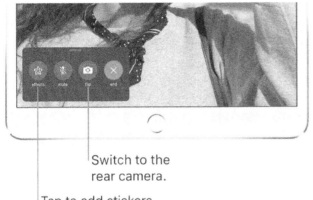

Switch to the
rear camera.

Tap to add stickers
or other fun effects.

❖ In the FaceTime application, tap on the Add icon
✛ at the top of your display.

❖ Write the person's number or the name in the
search box, then touch the Video call key⬜◁, or
press the audio call key ✆ .

Begin a FaceTime call from a Message chat

In a message chat, you can begin a call with the
individual you are conversing with.

- ❖ While chatting with the person, click on the name, My Account icon, or profile image at the top of the conversation.
- ❖ Click Face Time.

Take live picture while on a FaceTime call

When you make a video call with the FaceTime application, you can take a FaceTime Live Photo to snap a moment of the call. The camera snaps what happens before the shot is taken and after the shot, as well as the sound, so you can see and hear it.

To snap a FaceTime Live picture, first ensure the Face Time Live photo is activated in the setting application> FaceTime, then do any of the below:

- ❖ While having a call with another individual: press the live photo icon ○.

Tap to take a Live Photo.

❖ While having a Face Time group call: touch the tile of the individual you plan to snap a picture of two times, tap on the Full-Screen icon ↖ , then touch the live Picture icon ○ .

The two of you would get an alert that the picture was taken, and the live picture is stored in the Photo application.

Make a FaceTime group call on your iPad

In FaceTime, you can invite up to 32 individuals to a FaceTime group.

❖ In Face Time, tap on the Add icon + at the top of your display.

❖ Enter the name or number of people you want to call in the box above.
   You can tap on the Add Contacts icon to open contact and then add someone.

❖ Press the video key 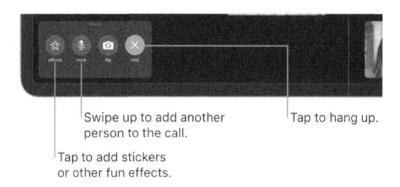 to make a video call, or press the audio button ☏ to make a FaceTime voice call.

Swipe up to add another person to the call.

Tap to hang up.

Tap to add stickers or other fun effects.

Everyone participating in the call would show in a tile on your display. When a participant speaks (orally or using sign language) or you click on a tile, the tile moves and becomes prominent.

Add someone to the group facetime call

Any participant can add another person at any time while the facetime call is going on.

❖ During a FaceTime call, touch the screen to display the facetime controls (if not visible), swipe from the top of the control, and then click the Add Person button.

❖ Enter the phone number, Apple ID, or name of the individual you plan to add.
Otherwise, click the Add button to add one of your Contacts.

❖ Click the Add person button on FaceTime.

Leave a Call

To opt-out of a call, tap on the leave Call icon ⊗.

Use the memoji feature

In the Message application, on your iPad, you can create a Memoji to use with your FaceTime calls. The iPad captures your gestures, facial expressions, and voice and transmits them to your memoji character.

❖ While a FaceTime call is going on, click the effects button ⊛ .

❖ Click the Memoji button ⬤, and select a Memoji

The other person in the call would hear what you are saying but sees the Memoji talking.

Change your looks with a filter

❖ While a FaceTime call is going on, click the effects button ⊛.

❖ Touch the Filters icon ⬤ to launch the filter catalogue.

❖ Change your appearance by clicking on the filters below.

Add a text label

❖ While a facetime call is going on, press the effects button ⊛.

❖ Click the text key ⬤, then click on a text label. Swipe up to see more text labels

- ❖ After selecting a text label, write the text you want to show in the note, then tap away from the text.
- ❖ Pull the label anywhere you want it.
- ❖ Touch the tag then touch the remove icon ✕ , to delete the tag.

Switch to the back camera

While the call is going on, click on the screen (if you don't see the controls), click on the switch Camera button 📷 (press again to return to the front-facing camera).

Turn the sound off

While the call is going on, touch your screen (if you do not see the controls), then press the Silent button 🎤 , tap on it once more to unmute.

Leave a call

Click on the screen, then press the Outgoing Call button⊗ .

Block unwanted FaceTime callers on your iPad

You can block voice calls, FaceTime calls, and text messages from unwanted callers in FaceTime.

❖ Enter the Setting application, and tap on FaceTime after that tap on Blocked contacts.
❖ Scroll down, and touch the Add new icon at the bottom of the catalogue.
❖ Choose the contact you are planning to block.

To unblock a person, simply swipe left, and press the unblock button.

FIND MY

Before you would be able to utilize the Find My application you have to configure location sharing.

Set up location sharing

❖ In the Find my application, Click on me and then activate **share my location**.
The device that shares your location will show under My Location.

❖ If the iPad doesn't share your current location, click on utilize this iPad as my location.

You can also change your Location settings in the Settings application click on [your name] then tap on Find My.

Create a tag for your location

You can set a tag for your current location (such as Home or Work) to make it more meaningful. When you click on **Me**, you will see the tag as well as your location.

- ❖ Click on **Me**, then click on Edit Location Name.
- ❖ Choose a tag.

  To add a new tag, click on add a Custom Label, type a name, and then click on done.

Share your location with your friends

- ❖ Tap on people.
- ❖ Scroll down the list of people, then tap on share my location.
- ❖ In the To field, type the name of the individual you plan on sharing your location with (or click the Add Contact button⊕ and select a contact).
- ❖ Click the send icon and select the timing of your location sharing.

Stop sharing your location

- ❖ Stop sharing with your friend: Touch **people**, and then click on the name of the individual you no longer want to share your location with. Then click on **Stop sharing my location**.

❖ Hide your location from everybody: Click on **me**, then deactivate **Share My Location**

Answer location sharing requests

❖ Tap on people.

❖ Click on the Share button under the individual's name that sent you the request, and select the timing for the location sharing, or tap cancel if you are not interested

Ask to see the location of a friend

When you share your location with your friends in the Find My Apps app, you can tell them to allow you to see their location on a map.

❖ Click on people, after that touch on the individual's name.

If you can't see someone's name, ensure your location is been shared with them.

* Click on Ask To Follow Location.

  Once your friends have received and accepted your request, you can see their location.

Remove a friend

If you remove a friend, that person would be removed from your catalogue of people and you would also be erased from their catalogue.

* Click on people, and then click on the name of the person you want to remove.
* Click Remove [name], click the Remove button.

Add an iPad to Find My

If you want to find your iPad with the Find My application if it gets lost, you must first connect your device to your Apple ID

The iPad also has an Activation Lock feature that prevents other people from activating and making use of the device, even if it is erased completely. To add your iPad

❖ Launch the Settings application> [your name]> then click on Find My.

Fill in your Apple ID if you are told to login. If you do not have, click on **Do not have an Apple ID or forgotten it?** then adhere to the directives on your display.

❖ Click on Find my iPad, then activate Find my iPad.

❖ Activate the following:

• Enable Offline Finding or Find My network: If your device is not online (not connected to Wi-Fi or mobile), Find My can find your device by making use of the find My network

• Send the last location: If your battery level is too low, the location is automatically sent to Apple.

See a device location

Utilize the Find My application to find and play sounds on your missing device (iPhone, iPad, iPod, Mac, Apple Watch, or AirPods). If you want to find a device, you need to activate the Find My Device feature before you lose it.

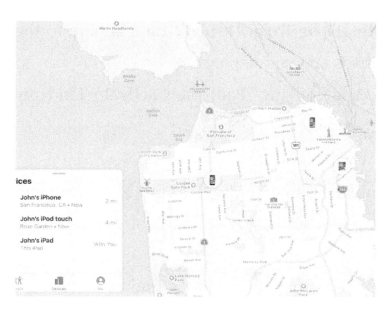

Click on the device you want to find in the device list.

❖ If you can find the device: it would appear on the map so that you can get the location of the device.

❖ If a device cannot be found: You see "location not found" beneath the name of the device. Activate **notify when found**, under **notification**. You will get an alert as soon as it is found.

Play sounds on Apple Watch, Mac, iPod touch, iPad, or iPhone

❖ In the devices catalogue, touch the device you want a sound to play on.

❖ Click on **play a sound**.

• If the device is online: the sound would begin to play for around two minutes.

• If the gadget is not online: you would see pending beneath play Sound. The note is played whenever the device is connected to a WiFi or mobile network.

After finding the device you can stop the sound before it automatically turns off by pressing the power button or any of the volume keys. If the device is locked simply unlock, or swipe to close the find my device alert

Receive directions to a device

You can get a device's current location from the Maps application.

- In the device list, click on the device you want to receive directions to.
- Click on the **Directions** to launch the maps app.
- Click on the route to find the location of the device.

Mark a device as lost in Find My iPad

Utilize the Find my application to mark your Apple devices as lost so no one else can access your personal info.

Add a custom message with your phone number.

Once your device is marked as lost, the following happens:

❖ An email would be sent to your Apple ID email.

❖ You can show a customized note on the lock screen of your device. For instance, you can write that you have lost the device or ways to get to you.

❖ Your device does not show notifications or make a sound when you get a message or notification or when the alarm goes off. Your lost device would still be able to get Face Time calls and phone calls.

❖ Apple Pay would be deactivated for that device. Any debit or credit cards setup for Express Transit cards, student cards, and Apple Pay would be erased from the device.

❖ For iPhone, iPad, iPod touch, or Apple Watch you will see on your map the current location of your device on the map application and any changes in the location.

If your gadget gets stolen or is lost, you can activate Lost Mode for your iPod touch, Apple Watch, iPhone, or iPad, or lock your mac.

❖ Click on devices, then touch the lost device on the catalogue.

❖ Click on the **activate** option under Mark As Lost.

❖ Adhere to the guidelines on the screen:

  • Password: If your device does not have a password, you would be told to create one. For Macs, you need to generate a numeric code, even if the Mac already has a password. This password is not the same as your passcode and is only used after marking your device as lost.

- Contact info: If you are asked to enter a phone number, enter the number you can be called with. If you are told to type a note, you can state that the device is lost and ways to reach you. The numbers and messages appear on the lock screen.

❖ Click on activate or Lock (for Mac).

Change the message or email notification for a lost device.

You can change your contact info or your email notifications after you've marked your device as lost.

❖ Click on device, touch the lost device from the catalogue.

❖ Under mark as lost, click on Activated or Pending.

❖ Do one of the below:

- Edit lost mode message: change your number or the note.
- Get email update: activate get email updates if it is not active already.

❖ Click on Done.

Turn lost mode off

After finding your missing device, do one of the following to disable Lost Mode:

❖ Enter the passcode on your device.

❖ In Find my, click on the device name, under Mark As Lost, click on turn Mark As Lost off, then click on Turn off.

Setup your AirTag

There are two main ways to setup your AirTag on your iPad. First, you can take your AirTag out of the box after removing the plastic cover and removing the last part from the battery compartment. Once you do that, it would display on your iPad just like AirPods.

The other method is through the Find My application. below are the two means:

How to setup the new AirTag on your iPad

❖ Go to your iPad's Home Screen

❖ Remove your AirTag from the box.

❖ Remove the AirTag from the plastic, being careful to gently remove the last plastic from the battery compartment. You would hear a sound.

❖ Press the connect button on your device.

❖ Select a name for the AirTag or enter a unique name.

❖ Click to continue.

- ❖ Click on continue after viewing your Apple ID
- ❖ Click on view in the Find My application or click on done.

How to setup AirTag in the Find My application

- ❖ Launch the Find My application on your iPad.
- ❖ Click on items.
- ❖ Click Add New Item.
- ❖ Click on Add AirTag.
- ❖ Click on the Connect button
- ❖ Select a name for the AirTag or enter a unique name.
- ❖ After reviewing your Apple ID information, click on the Continue button. Your device will now setup your AirTag.
- ❖ Click on done

See more info about your AirTag

If you setup your AirTag with Apple ID, you can find more information about it in Find My application.

❖ Click on items and click on the AirTag you want to see more info about.

❖ Do any of the below:

- Check the battery level: The battery icon shows under the AirTag location.

- Check the serial number: Touch the battery logo to view the serial number.

- Check the version of the firmware: Click on the battery icon to see the version of the firmware.

Find an item with AirTag

You can utilize the Find My application to search for AirTag signed in with your Apple ID.

In the Find My application click on item and then click on what you want to find.

- If the object's location can be found: it shows on the map so that you can see its location. The updated place and time appear beneath the name of the item.

- If the object cannot be found: You can see the place and the time it was last found. Activate **Notify When Found** under Notification. You will get a notification as soon as it is rediscovered.

Play a sound on AirTag

If the item is close, you can play a sound on it to help find it.

If you cannot play the device, you will not see the Play button.

- ❖ Click on **item** and then click on the item you want a sound to be played on.
- ❖ Click on **play sound**.
  Click on Stop Sound, If you want to stop playing before the sound automatically ends.

Receive direction to an object

Using the Maps application, you can receive directions to the current location of an object or the location last known.

❖ Click on the **items** button, then click on the item you are looking for directions to.

❖ Click on Directions to launch the Maps application.

❖ Click on the route to receive direction to the objects location from your location.

FACE ID

Use Face ID to open your iPad safely, confirm purchases and payments, and access third-party applications with just a glance at the iPad. You have to set a password on your device to use Face ID.

Configure Face ID or add another appearance

❖ If you did not set up Face ID the first time you set up your iPad, head over to the Settings application then click on Face ID & Passcode, after that tap on setup Face ID, then adhere to the guidelines on the screen.

❖ To set an alternate appearance, open the Settings application, then click on Face ID and Passcode, after that tap on setup an alternate appearance, then adhere to the guidelines on the screen.

Deactivate Face ID Temporarily

Face ID can be temporarily disabled from unlocking your device.

❖ Long press the top button and any of the volume keys for 2 seconds.

❖ Once the slider appears, press the top button to lock your iPad immediately.

The iPad automatically locks when you do not tap on the screen for about 1 minute.

The next time you open the iPad with your login code, Face ID would be reactivated.

Turn Face ID off

❖ Head over to the Settings application, then tap on Face ID and passcode.

❖ Do any of the below:

• Deactivate Face Id for certain items: turn one or more options off: Apple Pay, iPad Unlock, iTunes, and the Application Store or Safari AutoFill.

• Deactivate Face ID: Click on the reset Face ID button.

SAFARI

With Safari, you can browse the Internet and add web pages to your reading list to read some other time and add page icons to your Home screen for easy access.

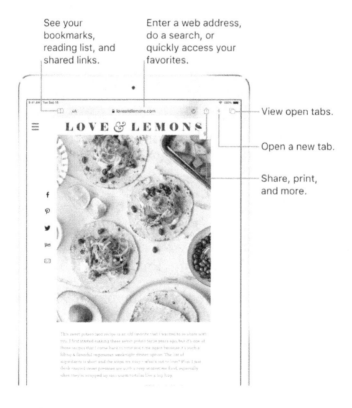

See your bookmarks, reading list, and shared links.

Enter a web address, do a search, or quickly access your favorites.

View open tabs.

Open a new tab.

Share, print, and more.

If you sign in to iCloud on all of your devices with the same Apple ID, you'll be able to see the pages you open on other devices, as well as keep your history, reading list and bookmark up to date on all of your devices.

View sites using Safari

You can navigate a page easily with a few clicks.

❖ Go back to the top: tap on the top edge of your display two times to go back to the top of a long page quickly.

❖ To see more about the page: Rotate your iPad to Landscape Orientation.

❖ Refresh a page: click the refresh button ↻ in the search box.

❖ Share an address: click the share button ⬆

Resize text, and change site settings

On the iPad, Safari features a desktop version of a website that expands for the iPad display.

Increase or reduce the size of the text, enter Readers view, define privacy restriction, etc. with the View Menu.

Click on the AA button in the left part of the search box to open the View menu, then do any of the below:

❖ Resize the font-size: Press the large A to increase the size of the font, or click on the small A to reduce the size of the font.
❖ View the site without advertisements or navigation menus: Click Reader View (if available).
❖ Hide the search box: click on Hide the tool bar (click on the top of the screen to display it again).
❖ See the mobile version of a page: click on Request mobile website (if any).
❖ View privacy controls and display whenever you visit this site: Click on website setting.

View two sites in Split View side-by-side

To open two web pages side-by-side in split view, simply follow the directions below.

❖ Launch a blank page in split view: press and hold the Page button ⬚, then click on open a new Window.

❖ Open any link in split view: long-press the link, and then touch Open in New Window.

❖ Pull the window to the other part of Split View: long-press the window top, pull it to the right or left.

❖ Close split view: pull the split view divider over the window you plan on closing.

Translate a page

If you come across a site in a different language, you can utilize Safari to translate it to a language you understand.

When you find a site in another language, click the Page Options button AA and click the Translate button .

Manage downloads

Click the download button to view the status of the file you are downloading.

Use keyboard shortcuts

You can also navigate through Safari by making use of keyboard shortcuts on the external keyboard.

Hold down the command key to see the available shortcut.

Bookmark a page on your iPad

Bookmark webpages in Safari then add them to Favourites to revisit them easily some other time.

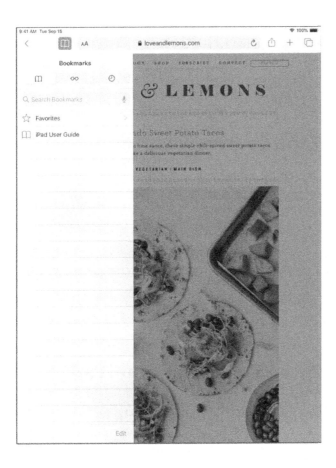

Bookmark the page you are in

Press and hold the Notes button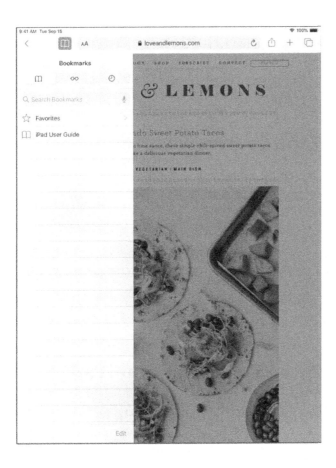, then click on the Add Bookmark button.

Bookmark open tabs

Long Press the bookmark button📖, then click on add bookmark for (number of) Tabs.

View and organize your bookmarks

Touch the bookmark icon📖, then touch the bookmark tab.

Click Edit to create or delete a new folder, rename it, or reorder the bookmarks.

View your Mac bookmark on your iPad

Head over to the Settings, then click on [your name], after that click on iCloud, then activate Safari.

Note: you must have also selected Safari in Cloud preference on your Mac and logged in with the same Apple ID.

Add a page to your Favourites

Open the page, click the Share button ⬆, and then click the Add to Favorites button.

Click the Notes button 📖 to edit your favorites, then click on the Bookmark tab, click on the Favorite button, and click Edit to delete, edit, or organize your favorites.

Quickly view your favorite and most visited pages

Click the search box to view your favorites. Scroll down to view frequently visited pages.

Note: To stop seeing a list of these pages, head over to the Settings application, then click on Safari and turn off frequently visited websites.

Add a site icon to the Home screen of your iPad

You can add a web page icon to the iPad Home screen to quickly access that page.

From the site, click the Share icon ⬆, and touch add to Home screen.

The icon will only appear on the device you are adding it to.

Save webpages to the reading list in Safari

You might find interesting things in Safari that you might want to revisit some other time, well you can save them in your reading list to make It easy for you to revisit later. You can even save items on your reading list to iCloud and read them when you're not connected to the Internet.

Add the webpage you are in to your reading list

Click the Share button ⬆, then click on the Add to Reading List button.

To add a link of a page without opening the page, long press the link, then click on the Add to Reading List button.

Look at your reading list

Click the Bookmarks button ☐, then click the Reading List button ◯◯.

To remove an item from your reading list, just swipe the item to the left.

Automatically save items on your reading list to iCloud for offline reading

Head over to the Settings application, then click on Safari, after that activate Automatically Save Offline (under reading list).

View privacy report

You can view the privacy report and modify the settings in the safari application to protect your browser activity from malicious websites.

Safari prevents trackers from following you when you are online. You can browse the privacy report to see a summary of sites that have been trying to track you.

To view the Privacy Report, click the Site Options button AA on the left part of the search box and click the Privacy Report

Manage privacy and security for safari on your iPad

Head over to the Settings application, then click on Safari, then under the Privacy and Security section, activate or deactivate any of the below:

❖ Block cross-site tracking: Safari restricts third-party cookies and information. Deactivate this option to permit cross-site tracking.

❖ Block cookies: activate this option to stop sites from putting cookies on your iPad. (To clear the cookies on your iPad, head over to the Settings application, then click on Safari after that tap on clear History & websites data.)

❖ Fraudulent site Warning: If you visit a website that is suspected of being fraudulent, Safari will issue a warning. Turn off this option if you do not want to be warned about fraudulent sites.

❖ Check Apple Pay: sites that utilize Apple Pay can check if you have Apple Pay on your device. Disable this option to prevent the sites from checking for Apple Pay.

When you visit a page that is not secure using Safari, a warning appears in the Safari search box.

Delete your browsing history and information

Head over to the Settings application then click on Safari after that tap on History & website information.

Accessing websites without creating history

Click the Page button 🗗, then click the Private button. If the private browsing mode is on, the background in Safari will be black rather than white, and the websites you visit are not listed on the iPad in History or on your other devices.

To hide the pages and exit Private Browsing, click the Page button 🗗 and then click the Private button once more. Web pages appear when you use the private browsing mode again.

MESSAGE

In the messaging application, you can send messages as MMS/SMS to anybody, or using iMessage you can send messages to people using iPhone, iPad, iPod touch, or Mac via Wi-Fi or mobile service.

iMessage texts may contain pictures, videos, and other information. You can see when someone else is writing and you can send a read receipt to let them know when you read your message. For security reasons, messages sent via iMessage are encrypted before been sent.

Login to IMessage

❖ Head over to the Settings application then click on Message.
❖ Activate iMessage.

Send messages on your iPad

Utilize the Messaging application to send.

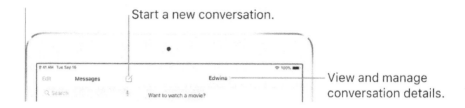

Start a new conversation.

View and manage conversation details.

❖ Click the Compose icon⬜ at the top of your display to begin a new message.

❖ Enter the name of the contact, Apple ID of the recipient, or phone number, or click on the Add icon⊕, and select from your contact list.

❖ Click on the text box, enter the message you have in mind, and touch the Send icon.

Pin a conversation

You can pin a certain conversation to the top of your Message catalog so that the persons you always contact are at the top.

Do any of the below:

- ❖ Swipe a conversation to the right, after that click on the Pin button 📌.
- ❖ Long press the conversation and pull drag it to the top of the catalogue.

To unpin a conversation simply long-press the conversation then tap on the unpin icon 📌 or long-press the conversation then drag the message to the end of the list.

Respond to specific messages in a conversation

You can reply to a certain message to improve your clarity and help keep the conversation going in an organized manner.

- ❖ Tap a message two times (or tap and hold the message) in the conversation, and then click on the Reply icon ↩.
- ❖ Type your answers, then click the Submit button ⬆.

Mention a person in a conversation

You can mention other people in a conversation to highlight a specific message. To do this, simply write @ before the person's name.

Send photos or videos

❖ While typing a message, do any of the below:

- Snap a picture within messages: press the camera button, then tap on the Capture button○ to take the picture.

- Record a video in a message: press the camera button, select the Video mode, and then tap the Video record button ◉

- Select an existing picture or video: click the Photos button in the app drawer, move left to view the next photos, or click All Images.

❖ Click on the Send icon or the Delete icon.

Send a voice message

❖ To send an audio message in a conversation, press and hold the Audio Record button ⬤ .

❖ Click on the **Play Message** button ▷ to listen before sending your message.

❖ Touch the Send icon or the Delete voice memo button to delete it.

Note: If you don't click the keep button in two minutes after you listen to the voice note, the iPad would automatically delete the message in order to save space

Create your own Memoji

Use the Messages application to present yourself with a custom Memoji sticker pack that suits your mood and personality. You can create your own Memoji - you can choose the color of it skin, its hair style and the colour, face, headgear, glasses, etc. You can create many Memoji for different moods.

❖ While in a conversation, click the Memoji Stickers button , then click the add New Memoji button ⁺ .

❖ Click on each feature and select the types you want. When you add features to the memoji, the character comes alive.

❖ Touch the done icon to put the memo in your collection.

To edit, add or delete a Memoji, click the Memoji sticker button ⬤ , click Memoji, and then click More Options ⋯ .

Send your Memoji and Memoji sticker

The message creates a sticker based on your Memoji and the characters of your Memoji. You can utilize stickers to display your emotions in a new way.

❖ Click the Memoji Stickers button ⬤ while in a conversation.

❖ Click on a Memoji in the row to see the stickers on the stickers pack.

❖ To send any sticker, do any of the below:

• Click on the sticker, Add a comment if you like, click the Send button to send.

• Click and hold the sticker, then drag the message into the conversation.

Send Memoji animated or recordings of Memoji

❖ Click on the Memoji button while in a conversation then select any Memoji.

❖ Press the Memoji Record button to record your expression and voice.

Click the Replay button to play your message before you send it.

❖ Touch the Send icon or the delete button to cancel.

APPLE PAY

Setup Apple Pay to make secure payments on applications and sites that support Apple Pay.

Add a debit card or a credit card

❖ Head over to the Settings application then click on Wallet and Apple Pay.

❖ Click on the Add Card button. You may be asked to sign in using your Apple ID.

❖ Do any of the below:

- Add new card: Place your card in front of the iPad so that it would show in the frame or enter your card details manually.

- Add your previous card: choose the card that is associated with the Apple ID, the card you utilize with Apple Pay on other devices, or the card you removed. Click the Continue button, then enter the CVV card number.

View card information and change the cards settings

❖ Head over to the Settings application then tap on Wallet and Apple Pay.

❖ Click on any card, then do any of the below:

- Click on Transaction to see your latest history. Turn Transaction History off to hide this info.

- Check the concluding four numbers of your card number and the Device account number.

- Edit your billing address.

- Delete the card.

Change the settings of your Apple Pay

❖ Enter the Setting application and Touch Wallet and Apple Pay.

❖ Do any of the below:

- Setup your default card.

- Add the address for shipping and the contact details for purchases.

NOTES

Utilize the Notes application to draw or write with the Apple pencil or your fingers. You can select from different Markup tools and colours and you can draw a straight line using the ruler.

Draw a picture or write in a note

❖ Start to draw or write in the note using the Apple Pencil. Or Click on the Manuscript button Ⓐ to draw a picture or write with your finger.

❖ Do any of the below:

- Switch colours or materials: Use the note tool.

- Change your handwritten text to a typed text as you write with the Apple Pencil: Click the handwriting tool (on the left side of the pen), and then start to write.

Add pictures or videos to note

❖ Click on the Camera key 🔲 in a note.

❖ Select an image or video from the photo library, or capture a new image or video.

❖ Long-press an attachment, then click on large image or small image to change an attachment preview size.

Tip: To draw on a picture, click on the image, then press the **draw by hand** button Ⓐ.

To store pictures and videos you have taken in the notes application to the Photos application, head over to the Settings application click on Notes and activate **save to Pictures**

Scan a DOC into a note with the camera

❖ Click on the Camera button in a note, then select **scan document**.

❖ Set the iPad so that the document page shows on your screen; The iPad automatically takes the page.

To snap the page manually, click on the **Take a picture** button◯ or the volume button.

❖ You can scan other pages, and touch Save when you are through.

❖ To edit the document you have saved, click on the document then do any of the below:

- Add more pages: Click the Add Scan button ⊕.

- Crop the picture: Touch the crop icon ⊓.

- Use filter: Click the Show Filters button ☺, and then select to scan the page as a color, gray, or as an image.

- Rotate the image: press the rotate key ⟳.

- Markup the document: Click the Share button ⬆, click the Manuscript toolbar ⊘, and then use the Markup tool to add your signature.

- To delete a scan, click on the delete button 🗑.

Lock notes on iPad

In the Note application, you can lock a note using a passcode to guard sensitive info. Note makes use of a single password for locked notes in the account on all your devices (for example, your iCloud account).

You can utilize Face ID as a way to access locked notes; however, do not rely on Face ID as the only tool to open your notes.

Adhere to the guidelines below to Setup your password:

❖ Enter the Setting application and Touch Notes after that tap on Password.
❖ If you own more than one account, select the account.
❖ Type your passcode and add a reminder.
   If you want more help, you can activate Face ID.

Lock notes

You can just lock notes on your device and iCloud. You cannot lock notes with video, page, Keynote, number documents, audio, PDF, or notes that match other accounts. You cannot lock iCloud notes that have collaborators.

❖ Open the note, then click the Note Action button ⓘ.

❖ Click on Lock.

When you lock a note, the name will remain visible in the notes catalogue.

If you want to remove the lock from a note, click on the Note Action button ⓘ, and then click the Remove button.

TIPS AND TRICKS

Store places in My Guides

Once you find a location in the search field, click on it to open a card with possible third-party Guides with topics like famous hotels or best resorts. '. You can save these Guides in the new section in Favorites; click on See all here, then click the '+' button to create your own guide where you can add locations and images.

Look around in Maps

Look Around has been surprisingly smooth and clear so far, although only a few cities have been photographed. Click on the binoculars button that shows up at the upper right part of your screen when the area you are looking at is covered, or click on the link to look around your map.

Hide your private pictures

There is a quick way to hide your pictures in an album other than your current camera roll album.

To hide your images, launch the Photos application and click the Select button in the top right corner. Then, click on the images you want to hide and select the Share button at the lower-left of the screen. Choose Hide from the menu at the bottom of the display.

How to use mouse on iPad

If you want to connect a mouse to an iPad, you will need a Bluetooth mouse. Launch the Settings application then click on Bluetooth, ensure that the Bluetooth of your mouse is turned on, Select your mouse from the Other devices segment then adhere to the pairing guidelines.

How to keep your iPad screen on

As a rule, your iPad will automatically lock after two minutes, and if you don't use it for two minutes, the screen may go dark. To keep the iPad screen on for a longer time: launch the settings application then click on Display and Brightness after that tap on Auto-lock, select between 2, 5, 10, 15 minutes, and never.

How to make changes to what you can access when the iPad is locked

Launch the Settings application then click on Face ID and Passcode, scroll down to the **Allow Access when locked** segment. Activate or deactivate what you like.

How to speed up iPad charging

You can speed up your iPad charging process by Turning on Airplane mode, simply swipe down from the top right part of your device home screen and click on Airplane.

How to turn on or off the battery percentage in a battery line

Launch the Settings application then click on Battery after that activate or deactivate Battery Percentage

How to factory reset your device

- ❖ Launch the Settings application.
- ❖ Touch General.
- ❖ Scroll down and Touch Reset.
- ❖ Touch **Erase All Contents and Settings**.

* If asked, type your login code.
* Type your Apple ID passcode to delete your device and remove it from your account.
* Press the Erase button.

Allow the recovery process to continue - no more than a few minutes.

Using the floating on-screen keyboard

Sometimes the size of the virtual keyboard on the iPad screen can make it difficult to use. For example, if you have a larger iPad Pro, it may take up a lot of space on the screen and hide its contents. This can also be difficult if you hold the iPad in one hand and write to it with the other hand.

To activate the floating keyboard

* Launch the application you want to type in with the keyboard on the screen.

❖ Touch the editing window to bring out the on-screen text cursor and keyboard.

❖ Now utilize your index finger & thumb, to pinch inwards anywhere on the keyboard.

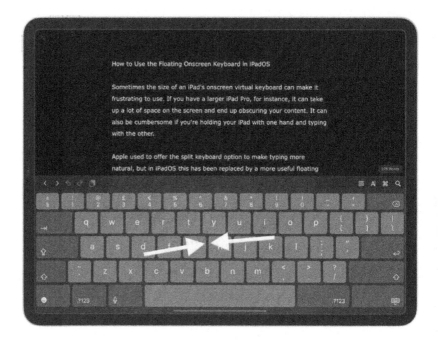

❖ The keyboard is reduced to the size of an iPhone keyboard. To move the keyboard to another area of your display, pull it there.

❖ To go back to full-screen size, just pinch outward

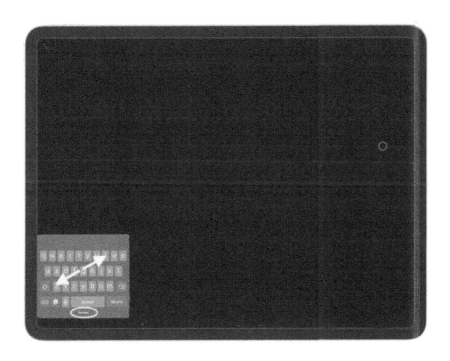

Another way to open the Floating Key is to hold down the Minimize keyboard button and click on the Floating button that opens.

Change Siri's voice

❖ Open the Settings application on your device.

❖ Choose **Siri and Search**.

❖ Select **Siri Voice**.

❖ Click on any option to listen to a demo of the voice.

❖ Check the Option you like.

How to access iCloud on iPad

iCloud is a cloud platform that serves all Apple devices. iCloud can store and sync all of your files, pictures, reminders, notes, and contacts and you can utilize it as your device backup.

iCloud keeps your content secure and keeps your applications up to date. This means that all information is secure and accessible on your Internet.

ICloud has 5 GB of free storage and more storage space can be added when needed. The 50 GB plan is

$ 0.99 per month, the 200GB and 2TB plans are $ 2.99 and $ 9.99 per month.

To access iCloud on your iPad, simply

❖ Open the settings application.
❖ Click on your name on the banner.
❖ Click on iCloud.
❖ Toggle the applications you want
❖ Scroll down and activate iCloud Backups.

How to access iCloud using a web browser

❖ Go to the iCloud.com website.
❖ When the screen opens, enter your Apple ID, and your login code.
❖ After signing in, you can utilize the iCloud application to access your information, documents, and photos.

Made in the USA
Coppell, TX
02 January 2022

70600591R00105